Signs

Lucy Ingrams holds an MPhil in creative writing from the University of South Wales. She has won the Manchester Poetry Prize (2015), the *Magma* Poetry Competition (2016) and the Ware Poets Prize (2018). Her debut pamphlet, *Light-fall*, was published by Flarestack Poets (2019). She lives in Oxford.

First Published in 2023

by Live Canon Poetry Ltd
www.livecanon.co.uk

© Lucy Ingrams 2023

978-1-909703-23-0

A CIP catalogue record for this book is available from the British Library.

Cover artwork: Pam Franklin

Contents

Acknowledgments

I am grateful to the editors of the following publications in which some of these poems first appeared : *Interpreter's House, Magma, New Writing Scotland, Obsessed with Pipework, Poetry Salzburg Review, Poetry Worth Hearing, Primers Volume One, Tears in the Fence, The Alchemy Spoon, The Hudson Review, Under the Radar* and *Ware Poets Anthology*.

Wayfaring

'To be pilot and stray.'   *Seamus Heaney*

What if you pulled in here, at this passing place – your mind-tide (of roof tiles
or tyre tread, inventories, bills) ebbs with the engine, lets through
a heart-skip : field knots and cloud-quilt toothed
all of a-piece, carding red July light.

What if drive-in panorama isn't enough tonight? If a wraith of the place
whispered you out – clambering car armour – to gate-climb a sign
that mugs 'camera surveillance'. And now you're swaying
in meadow-straw, stirring oat-husk and flies.

Say you made out, through the stalks, a wandering mark – just feinting
a track – and followed it. Up to the margin, then a dim tinder wood
that crackles 'old summer' (nothing liquid to hear – like a wren –
only pheasant shriek). You dip into, then

out of it. More stubble, more deer trail – under a moonrise. Everything
careless and frail, leached and combustible – which strips into your
glances, your thought-print, your pulse. When up stepped
a stile to you. Shows you lush rides (say you crane

over) tricked with guelder and sloe, council mown… What if you
refuse it (remembering fairy tales) but found alongside a slim
hairstreak way (moth-winged to a butterfly's). Rough-
tread its nettle and dock, bramble and loosestrife.

Deeper in … did you see it, the dry valley's secret? Spun with willow, buried
in oak : a river's gland seeping and pooling. Fresh to swim, dimped
with fish – studded with mossed ford stones you could cross.
What if you do, if you didn't—

blackbird's poem :

only   at the glamorous hour
                 violet   laundered in sheets
     across the lawns
  when pitch   leaks from the woods
                and moon-metal
         sharpens the cloud

at the mutable hour
      as windows stream   in the viscous air
  when flowers
        thin
         float out
             on the dark's slipways

what is it
    no thicker than a rabbit's listening
               presses back
     pushes the heart's sheath :   sound
           o p e n

"Hello from the children of planet Earth

where physicists today researched how many semi-
breves between a fall of chaffinch notes
and flocks of cloud resolving into rain. (And found
them equal to the crotchets of a poppy's wait
to open.) Yesterday, the southern sky dawned opal :
my mother's skin, peacock eyes of butterflies,
the river-mouth woke soft and lit ... roads rushed
lustrous traffic round. In stories here, the scent of love
is red – is rust, is roses. Do you tell a sound for war?
Those two slim words – two coin-sides – toss us ever
and over. I have not spoken of 'tonight' – which beats
a path to our tomorrows, always dark (thank you
in advance for your attention). It is the time
we think of you, in the minims between stars—"

after Voyager's *golden record greetings*
and Nina Mingya Powles

mommered

(dialect Oxon, Bucks)

to be confused
 in mind

to fold and un-
  fold lengths of
   cloth, newspapers

to take off
 a shoe, carry it

to sit barefoot, lift
 a cushion to
  the crown, wear it

to mistake a lamp
 for the moon, greet
  curtains as guests

to lock gazes
 and urgently enquire
  in mosaic languages

to do all this
 again, rims of your eyes
  pink with tiredness

to draw the interest
 of ghouls, palpable,
  knees up to their
   chins – counting

to ravel and un-
 ravel your loved
  ones (the feathered
   fright at my chest

yawing, useless as
 the flail of an un-
  tethered gate in a gale)

to mommer   to dement
 daze   flabbergast

Tree-fall

When I entered a wood in winter to shinny
 my gaze to the tips of trees, I couldn't keep
it there. Tracing a pattern of alder or a pale
 loft of poplar, low sun on black quarters
of yew, it would snag and drop back again.   Which

was the wood's way of telling its January : snow-
 fall these firs had succumbed to (seductive snow
that flew softly in flakes but lay more densely
 than softwood), storm-whips that hurled this high
beech bough (sky fluent and old-woman
 old) hair-down in the mud.   Going on

so, lowering / lifting my eyes, I sought
  to accommodate snags and hard weather (did
I reckon the wood must make the same reckoning?)
 till I came to a brake – this transom of oak
on the path, breached root pins tiptoeing air——   Awed,

floored as a mourner, I followed its lie, its
 giantness : moss sock, then arborglyph carvings (no
longer stretching a love), two woodpecker
 holes, whorled bosses (like fossils), the seam
of a lightning scar.   The young oaks

and I stood round, sensing a sawyer
 would come, while the wind dropped its toss
to the ground – drove leaf-ghosts in flocks
 that touched the bark-shroud as petals.   Through

the new funnel up to the cloud, a goshawk
 had lifted; slowly beat out the fresh circle.   Which
held my gaze shinnied, unsnagged
 and seeing / unseeing (as well as the bird) sheer
bushing crowns of a greenwood in summer.

In the half-light,

we stop to study the moor's winter shawl
  — tissue-crisp heather, leached moss, old grass straws —

when a rag of it sails loose, skims a camber of hill
  (floating not on the wind but its will)

settles back to where it settled before
  and knows something is new :

its wild sensor face, like a radio dish,
  yaws two hundred and twenty degrees

milling the twilight, listening for voles,
  then, hearing the feed of our watching-it too,

statues.   And now
  eons of eerie   unfold,

every pinprick of moor
  webbed in a spell

which we finally

                    break,

boots flinching home
  through the reach of its night-gaze.   Still

it stays still, moccasin-soft on its perch place,
  head-to-tail curved like a rind of new moon.

sentence

kairos ... an opening or 'opportunity'... through which
the archer's arrow has to pass.   *E.C. White*

midwinter work   to sit
out the afternoon   and sift
the rubble syllables   left
to you by illness   – threading and re-
threading sounds   listening
for messages

'foi foi acla' you laugh   'ooooh-
pe compy emmatary'   and slide
your hand to mine   'ohdy'
you sigh   then raise an eyebrow
'somethe why and tryan'
– this seems important

'I think so, yes' I nod   'I think
so too'   I've agreed this way
so often   which often
grates on you   you look me
over quizzically

*

the year's nadir   mid-
winter :   all day I've held
a lantern picture in
my mind   the bronze-age
horse in chalk   three
hills   or four   away   – that
works the seasons'
round   to pull the light
and draw time's   line
across the sky

*

'dee-kliton' now you tell
me 'formarosy' I smile too
widely   wildly fending off
a grief flare   — at dawn exactly
this solstice morning   the sun
rose   exactly horse-
back   to race the short
day breakneck

your grip   tightens on
my fingers   'I'll be al-
right, darling' — the fluent
sentence   passing   like
an arrow   through
an opening

*

I start   we stare
and meet   inside each other's
comprehension
                              and at
the window's instant   see
the light has   won the west
sinking pyrite   through the dark

Ship carver

Something about the coiled
  shavings that foam
at the door, the carver's
  crow's-nest gaze and the twisting
grain in a block of elm lays bare
  the chase between timber
and brine again.

Nor could the lift and swing
  of these workbench tools figure
anything but a choreography
  of care – to sharpen scrollwork,
dress a prow for the wind's
  hoops costs more than
a hobby's-worth of skill.

All this in a workshop keep
  seventy miles from
the tidemark. Day drains
  at the roof-glass to fill day
at the southern parallel
 and dusk closes over, swift
as the sea takes a skiff :

like coals, the piled sawdust gold,
  yellow-pine scents and the gleam
of the ship carver's mind
  ember a vigil. He will not fly,
as this angel from its stem head,
  whisking up salt spray, except
in thinking of it –

chisel   plane   bow-saw   chisel
  breath careful as a canary's under ground.

swimmer

the sea at light-
fall   fathom black
in a sheath of sky colour

the sea   the supple sea
at last light   flexing
unfathomably   beneath
its sleeks of pewter

      and you   half in   half
      out of them   rowing your
      swimming-hall crawl

in its element   confident   pitching
mostly in westerlies   spreading
evening-comfortable

   and there it lops and chops
   around the stacks, noses
   into bays and caves, periscopes
   up spies disguised as
   buoys of seal

   the was and is and will-be of its wash

the single sea   the source of anything
each cormorant   a piston
of its bird-thought   each fingerling
a pattern of its mackerel mind
easy   with that

   and here it mermaids
   gorgeously, sheers
   the flood tide in its
   basking silks

the is and will-be of its

the single source   of everything
air, its bubble   coast, its run-off – petrified
world's counterweight   its balance-tip
(cloud, the shadows of its rougher swells)
sorted   with that

       and you   back-stroking
       next   a flotsam speck   floating
       only at its pleasure

  the will-be of

and now the sea   the mawing sea
snuffs out day   exhales night

       and you   in negative   turned
       shadow in the star ash   racing
       to make land-
       fall

slow air

on a theme by Robert Burns

my
  heart   my
    heart's   my

in the moor-
  land   the mainland   the low-
    lands   the islands   the high—

my heart   my
  heart's not   my heart
    isn't

is chasing   is chaste for   is
  wandering   is wan
    for   wonders after

its dear,   and where-
  ever I   ever I
    go   go now,

my dear,   not to havens   to
  lochans   not to
    forests   to firths

my
  heart   my
    heart's   my

is near you   's never
  far from   isn't
    here

Signs

And whether you loved me   loved me not
 would come with a letter   come with you
would come   would come with some sign
 of which there was no sign   yet

and yet   when it came   a letter (not you)
 scribbled with signs   ceding your answer
I put it by on the table   walked out into fields
 hung with signs of their own   of spring breaking

through   wearing them naked as gooseflesh
 still   and looked for a text to hook yours to
red in the willow crowns   plum in the birch
 patterns of gnats   looked for a language

larger than us   *tremor of catkins*
 folds of a bud   for meanings like runes
harder than answers   *length in the light*
 the over and over of wood pigeon music

am out here still   waiting still longer   sure only
 I'm not   whether you love me   love me not
flowering stars on the blackthorn bars   *and at dusk*
 Sirius rising   Venus setting   or neither   and both——

Time-lapse to green

The first tree   to slip on a leaf dress   tries it
    shyly   arm-slenderly   reaching through icy air.

Her slipper is   rosettes of primula   new nettle tassels –
    her necklace   the bead-calls of kinglets   threaded by pines.

Sealed   like inscrutable urns   the bare trees still
    slow-dream   under their bark skins –

blind-stirring colour fields   (yellow parts
    summer / winter parts   blue).   Early

but too late to cancel   the first tree   (a hawthorn)
    gathers her snow shawl   a matchbook of catkins

scratch-starts a party   for one. Her drink   will be
    neat shots of sunlight   her song   a riff of west wind

and she'll dance   with a strong-headed nuthatch   (maybe)   till

    either   a milk of may-blossom   foams through
    or   the waking wood's   green   switches   on.

So will there be apples?

Cold nights   clear days   the fruit trees'
soft raised spurs   all thought of
him rinsed with light :   *promise me—*
and then?   the hedges whisper in
new viridian dialects   willow-wrecks
leaf into bird-houses   and
        she is distracted,

keeps coming up against singulars :   a
bicycling girl, her basket plaited
with hawthorn   *when will it rain?*
— it will *rain*   a blackbird's
tv-aerial aria   this blue match
to a log — flame licking
        the emerald evenings.

and now he is lost to her   if she looks for him
in the greenwood will she find herself
lose herself?   'frost in May'   her friends
are afraid for her   at what stage
of a fire is the term 'conflagration'
applied?   *so many promises*
        she goes out   she goes looking ...

how can anyone stand this much
tenderness,   the woods holding the last
of the day in their arms?   she wishes
a hawthorn bicycle, a path home   instead a
quiet fine rain begins :   *your promise*
— kept,   *so if I find you*   *will there be apples,*
        where now there are sleeves of blossom?

what if there's no further trace of him
    before nightfall?   the bird-houses
trip with alarm calls   her every step
        carefully—

Radio

When the turquoise radio arrived. Corner of the room. All the other angles
sharpening. Planes tautening. Not only that. The room's palette readjusts. As
a pantone swatch. Flickered through its wall whites / stitched bedspread reds /
wooden golds... It is night when the turquoise radio appears. The moon swims
at the glass dark to see.

When the radio's switch flicked 'on'. Tries the room's acoustic. Babbles tongues
and tones and notes. Unties silence— Clothes queuing near a basket (to wash /
to put away) sprawled further. As goers to a festival. And, listening from her
frame, a well-drawn girl hatched a dove from her forehead, hatches flocks.

When the radio arrived. Catching and throwing the whole room together. What
principle of motion / of magic lends it agency? Then the room flies into life.

August letter

In the dream you were – how were you? – whole, humorous, young. I must
write and tell you. Your skin shone.

I must write and tell you that I dreamt of you last night. And other news –
one friend makes her will, another plans his wedding for the spring.

It seems a time of year when people turn, address themselves. The moulting
birds too, empty the sky. Instead, colours move now on the wings of butterflies –
arguses and tortoiseshells cherish the eyes of asters over and over.

I want to tell you how the year to me from August appears upside-down, like a
tumbler tipped out. I peer into its tunc and trace a tiny counterpoint: snow hyacinths
on a tablecloth, winter coats on chairs pushed back, the smell of pears.

And I must ask you if you saw it too – perhaps our gazes met on its third eye –
last week's low-rise blue moon? In my dream, your look ran clear, ran green.

The evenings here are long still, are they with you? Yet I find I plant mine up with
candlelight, burn apple wood – watch the mirror catch and flush.

This month's like that, a flare I want to boost. That even so will carry summer out
upon its bier. My fingers flutter like the leaves to think of it.

In the dream, your hands were empty – full of your touch. If you were here, I could
put mine out and you could take them——

To shrimp

is to catch starfish, pipefish, hair-
weed, a sea stickleback, two hermit
crabs squatting winkle shells – instead

is to carry and keep upright
a bucket, for all the lather
and slip of wrack-sided rocks

is to be carried away – furbelows
or velvet horn, sea lettuce,
a breadcrumb sponge, their intricacies

is to play weather god, stirring
thunderheads over kelp-forests
with the plunge of each foot

is to Alice-up and uncomprehend
the pale blue gaze of islands
that come and go at the horizon

is breeze sky sea

is to dissolve between breeze sky sea
until living is only this twin-
tined wishbone :

        sweep of your arm /
        scoop of your net

is to forget to wish
even to harvest
your harvest

is brown shrimp   is glass prawns

Some things starlings are sensitive to :

each other

        wind

                cloud shadows

   hay bales

           Kestrel

      grubs

             people-pass

each other

       stubble-feel

            tractor-sound

     seeds

               wires

      worms

          rooks

              each other …

so that starling flocks are never still

    but blow all day, like the fields' leaves—

Blue hour

I walk out along the very line of land
       along the very keel of wind

  and through the stubble, flocks of grazing geese
  and on the shore, waders pick their feasts.

The west is cloud-in-pieces, sky-opera, inflamed,
the east is dim, even, opaque, gives nothing away

  and at times, a peregrine crosses latticely between
  and at times, the path unwinding hangs frail as a wire
                      sure as a stile between.

Viscous, livid, the last sun melts across the fields.
Sudden, twice-size, a red moon floats over the sea

and by illusion, I stretch my arms and seem to touch them both
and by eluding me, they seem, like gods, to talk above my head

    while what's fright   what's confidence
    what's loss   what's laughingness

    lie   as in a pan balance   still
    attended by the feeding of birds—

Till the minutes suck the light away
and the moon climbs grades of sapphire

and I turn and my step in the wind-drop quiet
is a thread to tack night
               to night.

عاله

Sonogram

from the mind of Sisyphus

<
>

We begin always in the dark
but while there is no end, there's no
monotony to the mountain's sides — me
and the boulder trace as many different
summits as a slug could silver

<
>
<

We will not clear the under-
world's abyss▐ but I'd swear that with
every fathomed brink a foot-candle of
earthlight steals across my back (newer
if no less cool than starlight)

>
<

Stars … the stars are much
of what I mourn, especially my star-
wife. *Condemned twice over — a widower
in hell.* Star-memory makes me maudlin.
The boulder's face glints back at me
— my tear-fall

>

… and there it
is, I'm not alone. I have, half
the time at least, my rock. (Remember
when the wizard Orpheus sang here?
The stone stopped short to listen
with me, offered itself as seat)

<
>
<

"No birds sing" in Tartarus. No-
thing grows. But at the peak, I rest
the feed of midnight, close my gaze. Below

the lids, colours marble into flower forms
from home : spurs of orchid and white
clover, tuffets of wild thyme. Some-
thing like a view

>

<

>

>

<

Never do we undertake descents
together. The rock in thrall to gravity's
desire... I keep a slower measure : walk
my fate back to its base. This is my
thinking time. (My thoughts are not 'heroic'.
There is a rhythm to it – is all.) And you get
good at guessing boulder cradles

>

<

<

>

Each time my calloused fingers
and the boulder touch again, a fresh
start breaks. To braille the mountain's
bulk – try to read beneath its scree
to fire-ore, to quartzes... What will our
knock, the effort of our patience, wake
one night inside its heap. What
change of state

<

>

<

Long drub

The sea is mumpish.
  It has a fever, an easterly.

A day, a night, another day,
  the dreich cast over won't shift.

The shore grows loud as a lay-by :
  we miss tractors, dogs, geese.

Spoondrift piles in the havens,
  suds about the villages, reaches the farms.

You think we're fine, but the bath
  runs over, softies burn.

I shout at the lights on the Stromness ferry,
  'Prettiest thing I've seen in a week——'

Brave : eider up the breakers like a lifeboat fleet,
  stiff-winged fulmar on the crunkling wind.

Afraid : a skylark's eye from the whins.

wind whip

along the wood's
  wandering
    edge :   not
  flowers ,   scrub

  wired   with stalks
 and thorn ,   husked
with last
    year's leaf

  no new leaf
either —   instead
  a tendered
      tenderness

              of
            catkins
           wagging
             from

              a
           hazel's
            wands

              and now
          this   saffron strobe
          — a siskin —   tangled
          in them   mingling
                golds

      tilu, tilu   *ti*—   the bird's
          sprung song   un-
              starts :

32

                                        a woken wind   is up

                        behind Bean Hill   soughs   seethes

                                        motorcades down

                the rides   bellows every web

            and twig   twists

                                    tugs

                                                    thugs

                            shakes

            shakes still

                        .

                        .

                        .

                        .

                        .

        dregged   in

    the silences it

    drags   are winter's

bets   — back on

                        from the ponds   stung

                    the raised cries   of geese

                        like   weals

A hearting space

'the hollow between two skins of wall.' *(dry stone walling terms)*

'Elsewhere we are as sitting in a place where sunlight
Filters down, a little at a time.' *John Ashbery*

He couldn't tell what his feelings were then : had formed instead a cairn-
making habit – small markers along the way raised from skirmishes
between his lived experience and his thought – hoping that one might
open soon : a door on to his unseen.

Walking in winter fields one afternoon, he'd watched his dog plant its hind
legs wide and tensile, as three deer bounced away from it – their pied,
plié-ing rumps synchronising in anticipation of the chase –

and it struck him, at once, that the trouble with story is that it has too
much gradient, is for ever tipping up or down hill, like those deer, turning
everything between into so much traction. *How to un-truck from it?* he'd
asked himself, as he spoke to his dog severely.

Later, she'd shown him a flock of waxwings flitch their way round a
berry-tree, ruthlessly light as they cropped it – and been drawn only
to a blackbird planted heavily nearby, witness to the attenuating dusk.

       Hey, hey? she'd asked,

so he'd explained about the tipping deer, and how he wondered if
the blackbird, unlike the dog, had un-coupled itself from story? How,
come to think of it, he'd felt attracted for weeks now to the floors of
valleys, level bodies of water, flat roofs, table mountains——

Next morning, he'd been tempted to call her in much the same vein : *Just
here, on the patio flags, where the neighbour's cat lies taking the January sun* ...
just here, something might show itself, a point of origin open...

But when the cat lifted its bedazzled head, he'd thought he read in the prick of its ears that this was no more than yearning on his part, and planted the phone back in its holster. (Whereupon it rang – and was someone else entirely.)

Whether from doubt, or the nature of the exercise, these cairns of his almost always stayed blind, though stray cracks of light shone on his increasing skill at placing dry stones. Even so, he resolved to keep raising them – doggedness being close to, if not actually, a feeling.

Apple

It was a blossom's idea
  — notional.
    Then a bee made it.

Rain, wind, sun turned it.
  Who knows what the moon
    taught it by night?

A branch's load,
  it grew to be load-bearing
    and carry the seeds of itself.

When it was ripe, it blushed.
  The scent it gave off
    distracted the horses.

A symbol of knowledge,
  it yearned to try
    gravity

        and

           fall—

It sits plump in this rut.
  It is waiting for thrushes and worms
    to get at its core.

A new order

'Out of the single night
came the day's look.' *John Berger*

A wind rose   with the light
  this morning   abrupt and sea-
sounding the wood,   threw the song-
  birds   who threw their voices   – so
dawn chorused   discordant,   turned
  willow rooms   inside out

by breakfast   it was still dragging
  the clouds around   like so many
nets of herring,   hayfields
  flattened,   festivals of butter-
cups   bent double   to examine
  their roots

though a poplar offered   a trillion
  leaf articulations   accommodations
and associations,   an ash   is shedding
  its sticks   and more things   tied
to each other   loosen and un-
  couple   (by noon   a beech will be down)

and look!   under the baleful half-
  stare   of a half-insomniac moon   eight
nine   raffish red kites   tack in   to helter-
  skelter on the currents,   while along
the hedgerow   ganging martins   dive-
  bomb every gust

and a bandit stoat   licensed by
  the birl   breaks its cover   towing
rabbit kits,   their cache-grave
  freshly dug   – the gale   faint
on the fade   of their listening,   their wind-
  pipes   paying out   breath——

37

Thinking with Goya's 'They Descend Quarrelling'

That rage lent them buoyancy seems
  natural : mid-quarrel so mid-
    air, and makes me think of you /

of me, how yesterday (again – so often
  now we reach the tipping-
    point where gravity for us

runs out) we switched the drag
  of borne resentment for the lift
    of hurled invective ...

and then of penalties – the way pay-
  back for an astronaut (for all that heady free-
    fall) comes in cosmic rays and solar wind ...

which touches on the guilt
  that Goya (still) can look straight
    through, as I remember

– from our venting-spot –
  how simultaneously
    we'd seen

the hive of our love's home /
  the ragged narrows
    we were plunging to ...

and on perversity : you'd hope
  that vision among fighters
    would inspire a thirst for peace

but we'd fought on – in spite –
  like children
    or the damned ...

which brings me face
  to face with why
    I'm grounded here

this late-night opening, among the careful
  optics of Goya and the gallery,
    not daring to go home——

                    So spare the ghoul woman
                and ghoul man – swinging
              just at the mind's height.

Front room

Along the thin mesh filtering two states
of the light. At the selfsame moment
the grey-water river shrugs off
its lustre, or a pipistrelle whets
her speed. When the room
begins to appear.

Which at noon was guileless. You'd
pass by unnoticing. But now –
as Wednesday commits *sati* at
its window – starts putting on
globe-flesh. Wears its few
choice ornaments like countries.

No lamps of its own. The door
to the room stands always
open to a sun-moon body –
the light in the hall. That deepens
with dusk. That spawns shadows, like
frogs, to lake over the floor.

If I could only show you : the curtain-
less room is exquisite. Lime-washed
to white. A dark mirror repeating
its uneven symmetry. Jars of
grasses, field flowers. Once, two
smoking mantelpiece candles.

Even if you walked in the street
backwards and forwards, forwards
and backwards, watching for hundreds
of years… The immaculate
room never holds so much
as a wasp.

Certain nights like this, as it
thickens with suggestion, its own
dense mystery. How often has it
hooked from me that rusted
wish, drowned deep off
my capes of good hope—

My selves in a wood

How was I messing in flushes and ditches
  outside all that time, when a few steps
in, every flyaway strand of me
  earthed, and (gentle) was sifted by slim
serried birch, slanted oak quiet.

The path – the path was a basket and carried
  us. Any bend, any rise and flanks
of field maple, sycamore, spindle crowded
  to meet us. *What's here and what's not*
was a question, for the wind swung
  far up in the wildwood's acoustic.

Nor can I tell why the grain of us
  shifting and settling sanely (these selves
of my self) stayed gated behind the wood's
  winter bars of spareness | slowness
straight-standing | straitenedness
  when that wasn't it.

Had we heard the little twists
  of birdsong thrown like sweets
between the trees, seen the bolts of gauzy
  sunlight loosed along the floor, snow-
drop republics declared
  among the pine cones—

I had only to touch the leaf scales
  callousing the beech and fingered
ash to reach it : spring's lick –
  its blistering quick – flame fed
from an ember in the heartwood—

You are lost, you are
walking out of the picture

When did it
happen, the slip,
exactly? You took
a turn there, a turn
here, like water's
winding, through
the unvisited wood
and now have
dropped into
your scare-
scape : heels
slowing as
the stretch thins
from home.

For sure, the birch
and beech boles
sheer straight up
still, arrows
to the wide air,
and through a shale
of shadows jam-
shine lustres from
the brambles, pine-
cones breathe,
a chicken-of-
the-woods looms
warm as torchlight –

yet this plunge
the wind comes
sometimes in
to stir, that's calving
(unsigned) paths,
folds you into

blindness more
and more — clear
landscape-maps
lie at every border
but inside here
is mute abstraction :
silences and time
in curves, the pulse-
tip leaves, densities
of dark multiply.

One flower,
low-growing,
flecks in
and out,
peripheral.
It wears
the feint
and shiver
of enchanter's
nightshade
and images
your dread — its
fraying deckle-
edge—

Cross-section of a moment   passing

And this my hobble   where the deer graze   or melt
  away   sharps of nettle after rain   my waiting

shaped like this :   four-cornered to a squat   set
  diamond   to the four-square field   my soles

turned ears   tuning for a key of drift
  and bedrock   — a kestrel locked in thrall

above.   Stillness   and the long
  quiet of ironstone   fire-dark and dream-scaled

reeks into   pores of brickearth   sighs
  slowly   to the surface

        colours   to a foam
         of dandelions   and ryegrass

now backcombed from the west by plunging light
now caught and held as glister in the falcon's eye